Camdean School

Item no.   00291

Safety in the Home

DOROTHY BALDWIN and CLAIRE LISTER

Safety First

Safety in the Home

Safety on the Road

Safety at School

Cover *Water and electricity are very dangerous together. Never handle plugs, switches or machines with wet hands.*

First published in 1986 by
Wayland (Publishers) Limited
61 Western Road, Hove
East Sussex, BN3 1JD, England

© Copyright 1986 Wayland (Publishers) Limited

British Library Cataloguing in Publication Data
Baldwin, Dorothy
Safety in the Home. — (Safety first)
1. Home accidents — Prevention —
Juvenile literature
I. Title   II. Lister, Claire   III. Series
363.1'375   TX150

ISBN 0—85078—908—7

Phototypeset by
Kalligraphics Limited, Redhill, Surrey
Printed and bound in
Belgium by Casterman s.a.

Contents

All words that appear
in **bold** are explained in the
glossary on page 30.

About this book

Have you ever cut yourself, or choked on a piece of food? Were you thinking about safety when the **accident** happened? Here is a list of the most common accidents in the home.

- Falls
- Cuts
- Burns and scalds
- Poisoning
- Choking
- Drowning

Some of these accidents happen when people forget about safety. Babies and toddlers have to be protected against accidents. But you are old enough to watch out for danger and so prevent accidents. *Safety in the Home* gives you the main danger spots to look out for.

A boy helps his sister to drink, to make sure she doesn't choke.

Falls

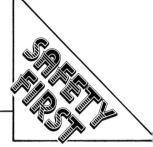

Where did you last fall down? Was it in the playground or on your way to school? Perhaps it was at home? More falls happen at home than anywhere else.

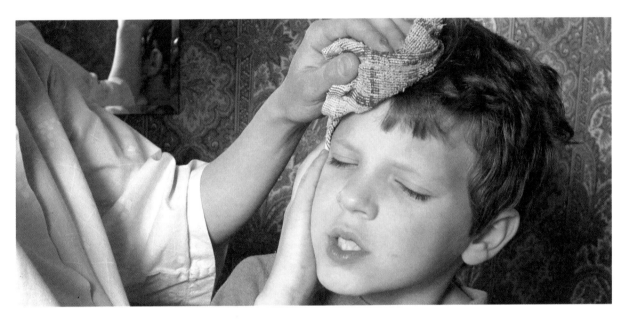

Falls can cause cuts and bruises.

Why do people have falls?

Babies fall over because they are not very good at walking. They like exploring and they do not know about safety. Children may trip over things when they get excited. They forget about safety.

Grown-ups sometimes fall if they are very busy. They may try to do too many things at once. They forget to look where they are going. Elderly people may get dizzy and fall if they move too quickly.

Danger spots!

● Floors: Watch out for spills on the kitchen floor. They can make it very slippery. Always mop up anything you have spilled. The bathroom and shower floors are often wet and slippery. A non-slip mat helps to prevent nasty falls.

Small rugs and mats can be slippery. Take extra care when you walk on them. Unless they have a non-slip backing, you may skid across the floor.

Study this picture of a bedroom floor. How many danger spots can you find? Trailing leads cause many falls, and so do toys, books and anything else left lying on the floor. Pick up your games when you have finished playing, and wind away any leuds, string or wool. Do this wherever you play — not just in your bedroom.

● Furniture: Are there any **swing doors** in your home? Do not rush through, someone may be coming the other way.

Look at the picture. Can you work out the different accidents that might happen? Tables and chairs should be moved away from the windows so that small children cannot reach them. If you climb up kitchen steps to reach something from a high shelf, ask a grown-up to hold the steps steady. Better still, ask the grown-up to reach up to the shelf for you.

● Shoes: Shoelaces can trip you up if they come untied. Are yours done up tightly? Do you use a double bow? Old slippers feel comfy, but they can be too loose and cause falls. New shoes may have polished soles and feel skiddy. Ask your parents to make them safe by **scoring** a few lines on the soles to take away the smoothness.

● Stairs: Some children like to play jumping games on the stairs. Lots of falls happen this way. At night, switch on the lights so that you can see where you are going. If the carpet is loose or worn, you can easily trip up.

Be careful coming down the stairs and keep one hand free to hold on to the banisters.

If there is a toddler in your family, never leave the stair safety gates open. It can be fun teaching a toddler how to climb up and down stairs safely. Did you know that it is more difficult to learn how to come down stairs than to climb up them?

Toddlers are unsteady on their feet and can easily fall, so make sure that stair safety gates are kept closed.

Cuts

You can cut yourself badly if you have a nasty fall. The main causes of other kinds of cuts are shown in the picture below. Which of these things should have been thrown away safely in a bin? Can you think of any other things which may cause cuts?

There may be some of these sharp and dangerous objects in your home or garage, so take care.

Safety and sharp objects

● Always cut things away from you — never towards you. Then, if the knife slips, you will not cut yourself. Try to learn this rule.

● Always pass a knife with the handle turned towards the other person — then neither of you need touch the sharp edge.

● Broken toys, especially plastic toys, have nasty sharp edges. Throw them away safely. Do not give them away. Can you guess why?

● Take extra care when you open a tin or lever up a bottle top. The edges can be terribly sharp.

● Always put empty bottles, empty tins and ring-pulls away safely in a bin. (Have you ever left one lying about?)

Some scissors are very sharp. For cutting-out games, use blunt scissors with rounded ends.

It is good for growing feet to run around without shoes, but watch out in the garden — there may be sharp things hidden in the grass.

● If you break a cup or glass, do not mop up the spilt liquid first. Some things smash into such tiny slivers that you cannot see them. Fetch a broom, or dustpan and brush, and sweep up the pieces you can see. Tell your friends to stay clear until a grown-up has checked there are no tiny slivers left. Then you can mop up any spilt liquid.

Pocket-knives

These are big danger spots. If you are given a pocket-knife, learn how to use it safely.

● Hold the handle firmly with the sharp side of the blade away from your body.

● Make sure the knife locks open before you use it, or it may snap shut on your fingers.

● Some pocket-knives are stiff and difficult to open and close. Do not use them.

● Never leave a pocket-knife open when you have finished using it. Can you think of one reason why? Close the blade by pressing the blunt edge with the **heel** of your hand.

When you carve wood, watch out for splinters.

Burns and scalds

Burns are caused by dry things such as fires, matches and cigarettes. Scalds are caused by wet things such as hot drinks, hot cooking oil, boiling water and steam. Have you ever had a burn or scald? They are very painful. You can stop the pain by holding the burned part in cold water for 10 minutes. It is better, of course, to take care and avoid accidents.

Never play around with matches. You may accidentally start a fire.

Burns

There should always be a safety guard around a fire.

Remember not to put clothes on storage heaters to warm or dry. There is a risk they will catch fire.

Never stand close to a fire in long loose clothes. Many children have been badly burned because their clothes caught fire this way.

Toys and 'interesting' things should not be left on the shelf above the fireplace. Toddlers may be tempted to reach up to them.

This girl's nightie could catch alight as she reaches to the mantlepiece. Always put a fireguard around a fire.

There are many danger spots in the kitchen. Can you think of three? Do not run around in the kitchen if someone is ironing or cooking a meal. Can you think why this would be dangerous?

Bonfire night is exciting, but no matter how carefully fireworks are made, a few of them always go wrong. Take great care at a firework party or barbecue and never play around with fireworks or matches. The burning ends can stick to your skin and go on burning.

A barbecue is fun, but remember to take care near the fire.

Before you have a bath make sure the water is not too hot. If there is a non-slip mat, put it in place to stop any falls.

Scalds
● In the bathroom: When you have a bath, turn on the cold tap before the hot tap. This cuts down the amount of heat and steam. Always test the temperature of the water before you get in.
● In the bedroom: Hot-water bottles sometimes burst and cause nasty scalds. If you feel cold at bedtime, jump up and down for two minutes. This warms you up and your bed will soon feel cosy from your body heat. If you have an electric blanket, it must be switched off before you get into bed.

● In the kitchen: The cooker is a big danger spot in the kitchen. Ask to be taught how to use it — never try on your own. Some cookers have a guard rail around the edge to stop small children touching the heat. Do you know why saucepan handles should always be turned to the back of the cooker so that they do not stick out?

In some countries, chips are a favourite food, but the boiling oil in which they are cooked is very dangerous. Keep well away from the cooker if someone is making chips.

Babies should be strapped into a high chair a little way from the table so they cannot touch hot plates and cups. Toddlers will try to pull themselves up by holding on to the edge of a hanging tablecloth. They do not understand how dangerous this is. Can you think why it is safer to use place mats instead of a tablecloth?

More than half of all scalds happen because hot liquids are passed over children's heads. Liquids spill very easily.

Machines save a lot of hard work, but they must be used carefully.

Most people have some of these machines in the kitchen:
- Cooker
- Coffeepot
- Dish-washing machine
- Food blender
- Iron
- Kettle
- Washing machine
- Toaster
- Freezer and/or fridge
- Microwave oven

How many of these machines are there in your kitchen? Can you think of some more?

Water and electricity are very dangerous together – an **electric shock** can kill! Never play around with machines. Small children should never be left alone in the kitchen when any of the machines are working.

Fire! Fire! Emergency!

In case of fire

- Dial 999 for the **emergency services**. Emergency calls are free so you do not need any money.
- Ask for the Fire Brigade.
- Give the telephone number you are ringing from.
- Explain what has happened and make sure you give the address very clearly.
- Do not put down the telephone until you are told to.
- Warn the people in the burning house, and tell all the neighbours.
- Never go into a burning building — wait for the Fire Brigade to arrive.

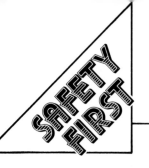

Poisoning

Medicines

A little medicine does you good but too much does you harm. It is strange to think that medicine is a **poison** if too much is taken.

Some medicines are kept in 'child-proof' medicine bottles. The top is made in a special way so that small children cannot open it. But some medicines may be in ordinary bottles, plastic bottles or boxes.

Pills often look like sweets. Some liquid medicines taste quite nice. Sadly, many small children are rushed to hospital each year because they have mistaken pills for 'sweets', or liquid medicines for 'drinks'.

These pills may look like sweets but they are dangerous drugs.

If you see any medicines lying about, put them safely away in the medicine cupboard or on a high shelf. Then they will be out of sight of your younger brothers or sisters and their friends.

Some children have to take medicine each day. They are very sensible about this. When they are at school they ask the teacher, or person in charge, to keep the medicine in a safe place.

Chemicals

Dirty clothes can be very hard to clean. Some pots and pans, kitchen sinks and drains can be hard to clean as well. Powerful chemicals are needed to get the dirt out. The picture below shows some of these powerful chemicals. They are poisons. Some will also burn skin and damage eyes if they are splashed or spilled.

Household cleaners and chemicals may be poisonous. Do not touch.

Other kinds of poison

Some homes use poisons to get rid of flies and other insects. These poisons are called **insecticides** and are dangerous. Do not touch!

Lead is a poison used in some pencils and paints. It should never be used in children's toys. If you go shopping for pencils and paints, find out if they are **'non-toxic'**. This means that they are made without poisons.

This boy makes sure he paints his models with non-toxic paint.

Do you use glue to make models? Do you use **'thinners'** to clean up any spilled paint? These are all poisonous. Take care not to put your fingers near your mouth while you are working. Make sure you wash your hands very well when you have finished.

Can you think of another time when washing your hands very well is important? Poisons can pass among people if just one person forgets to wash after using the toilet.

Grown-ups sometimes use empty bottles of squash to store poisons. This is very dangerous. Never take a drink from a bottle which looks dirty and old, or is kept in the wrong place.

Would you take a drink from an old bottle under the kitchen sink? The answer is no, of course not! If there is a toddler at home, all poisons and powerful chemicals should be kept on a high shelf.

Household cleaners and chemicals should not be kept under the kitchen sink. From the picture, can you see the reason why?

Choking

Have you ever choked on a large piece of food? Has water ever 'gone down the wrong way'? It makes you turn red in the face — you choke, splutter and cough.

Coughing usually brings up the large piece of food. A hard, sharp bang on the back also helps. Choking can sometimes be serious. People may die if food gets stuck in their throat.

At mealtimes, cut food into small pieces and chew it well.

Safety at mealtimes

● Cut large lumps of food into small pieces. This is especially important for toddlers, who do not have many teeth.

● Chew your food very well. Your side and back teeth are for chewing and grinding. Make sure you do not try to swallow any large lumps.

● Food and drink can 'go down the wrong way' if you talk or laugh as you swallow. Stay calm at mealtimes and try not to eat in a hurry.

Babies and toddlers

● Leaving your baby brother or sister alone with a bottle can cause choking. Always hold a baby when you give him or her a drink.

● Babies should sleep on their front or side – never on their back. This stops any **vomit** slipping down a baby's throat which may cause choking.

Never let a baby or toddler sleep with pillows. A pillow can smother a baby and stop him or her breathing.

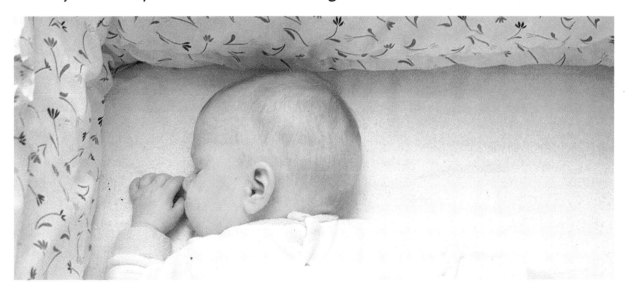

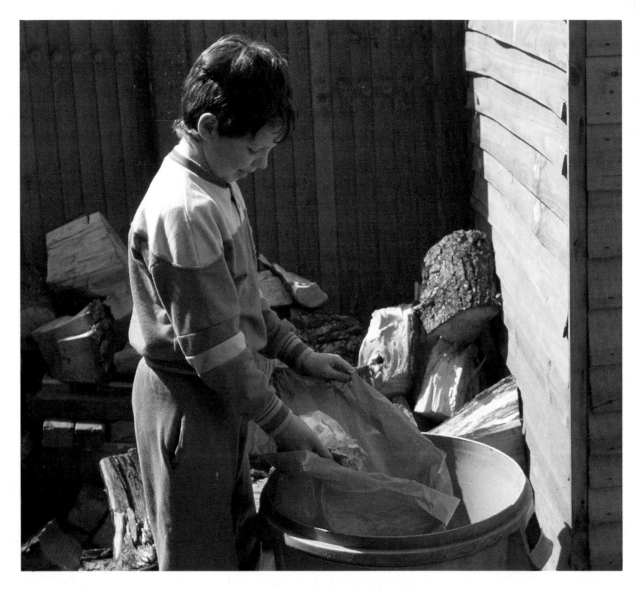

Throw away empty plastic bags and sharp things into a bin.

● Watch out for empty plastic bags. They are big danger spots. Toddlers like to pull them over their heads. They do not know that this can stop them breathing. Always put empty plastic bags away safely in the bin.

Drowning

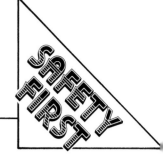

Babies can drown in 5 cm (2 in) of water. If you measure this on your ruler, you will see how very little it is. Never leave a toddler or baby alone near water. They can fall into it, and may not be able to lift their heads up for air. The paddling pool, the bath, even a pail of water is dangerous. You can have fun splashing with your toddler or baby in the water, but you must not leave them alone.

Never leave babies and toddlers alone near water.

Remember! You can help to prevent accidents in the home by watching out for danger. You may even save someone's life.

Glossary

Accident An event which happens by mistake, and sometimes causes someone to be injured.

Electric shock Electricity can be very dangerous. Someone who comes into contact with live electricity can be seriously injured and suffer from 'electric shock'.

Emergency A sudden event which needs immediate action.

Emergency services The Ambulance Service, the Fire Brigade, the Police Force and the Coastguard are all 'emergency services'. They can be called out to help in an emergency by dialling '999'.

Heel (of the hand) The part of the palm of the hand nearest the wrist.

Insecticides Special poisons used for killing insects.

Non-toxic Not poisonous.

Poisons Substances which can make you very ill if they are swallowed. Some poisons can kill.

Scoring Marking with lines, using a knife or other sharp object.

Swing doors Doors that can open both ways, by being pushed or pulled.

Thinners Liquids, such as white spirit or turpentine, that are used to dissolve paint.

Vomit The food in the stomach which is thrown up when someone is sick.

Books to read

Better Road Craft by Ted Bannister (Kay Ward, 1973)

First Steps in First Aid by Ian Roy (Ladybird, 1981)

Home Safety by Marjory Purves (Ladybird, 1981)

I Want to Cross the Road by Barbara Preston (Dinosaur, 1978)

Let's go Across the Road by Rachel Wise (Franklin Watts, 1980)

Road Sense by R. Collingridge (Ladybird, 1981)

Safety at School by Dorothy Baldwin and Claire Lister (Wayland, 1986)

Safety on the Road by Dorothy Baldwin and Claire Lister (Wayland, 1986)

Water Safety by R. Birch (Ladybird, 1981)

Picture acknowledgements
Colleen Payne 6, 7, 20, 21; Jennie Woodcock 4, 5, 11, 14, 15, 17, 18, 27, 28, 29; Tim Woodcock *cover*, 9, 10, 12, 13, 19, 23, 24, 25, 26; ZEFA 8, 16, 22.

Index